Travel Guide To Torrevieja 2025

Explore Authentic Local Spots Beyond the Tourist Trails

Jordan F. Green

Copyright © 2024 Jordan F. Green

All rights reserved. No part of this publication may be reproduced, distributed, or transmitted in any form or by any means, including photocopying, recording, or other electronic or mechanical methods, without the prior written permission of the publisher.

Table of Contents

INTRODUCTION

CHAPTER 1: GETTING TO KNOW TORREVIEJA
 1.1 A Brief History Of Torrevieja
 1.2 Geography and Climate.
 1.3 Cultural Insight

CHAPTER 2: ACCOMMODATION
 2.1 Top Neighborhoods to Stay:
 2.2 Recommended Hotels and Hostels
 2.3 Unique Accommodations: Guesthouses and Rentals

CHAPTER 3: AUTHENTIC LOCAL EXPERIENCES
 3.1 Traditional Marketplaces and Food Halls
 3.2 Community Festivals & Events.
 3.3 Local Arts and Crafts

CHAPTER 4: CULINARY DELIGHTS
 4.1 Must-Try Dishes: Where to Find Them

4.2 Hidden Gem Restaurants

4.3 Tapas Bars Off the Beaten Path.

CHAPTER 5: OUTDOOR ACTIVITIES AND NATURAL WONDERS

5.1 Exploring Natural Parks.

5.2 Beaches Less Traveled

5.3 Hiking and Bike Trails

CHAPTER 6: CULTURAL HOTSPOTS

6.1 Local Museums and Galleries.

6.2 Theatrical and Live Music

6.3 Historic Landmarks

CHAPTER 7: DAY TRIPS FROM TORREVIEJA

7.1 Nearby Towns to Visit 1. Orihuela

7.2 Scenic Driveways and Routes

7.3 Natural Escapes

CHAPTER 8: NAVIGATING TORREVIEJA

8.1 Public Transport Options

8.2 Walking Tours and Bike Rental

8.3 Tips for Moving Around

CHAPTER 9: PRACTICAL INFORMATION
    9.1 Safety Tips and Emergency Contacts
    9.2 Currency and Payment
    9.3 Language & Communication

CHAPTER 10: INSIDER TIPS
    10.1 Best Time to Visit
    10.2 Local Customs and Etiquette
    10.3 Sustainable Travel Practices

CONCLUSION

INTRODUCTION

Welcome to Torrevieja!

Torrevieja, located on Spain's southwestern coast, is a lovely seaside town that combines sun, sea, and culture. It is known for its beautiful beaches, dynamic environment, and rich history. While many tourists visit the well-known tourist attractions, this book encourages you to go beyond the traditional sights and find the true local experiences that make Torrevieja truly unique.

Torrevieja, which means "Tower of the Sea," has a unique history as a salt mining town. The salt flats, known as Las Salinas, are not only a background to the city but also an important part of its identity. The local salt industry has affected the area's culture, economy, and food. When you arrive, you will be attracted by the saline breeze, the colorful salt mountains, and the friendly residents.

In this guide, we hope to offer you the necessary information to navigate Torrevieja like a local. If you're looking for hidden restaurants, small markets, or gorgeous sites off the usual road, we've got you covered. Prepare to embark on an extraordinary adventure that will uncover the heart and spirit of this enchanting town.

How To Use This Guide:

This travel guide is intended to accompany you while you explore Torrevieja in 2025. It's divided into distinct parts, each focusing on a particular facet of the town, so you can locate the information you need quickly and easily. Here's how to make the best of it:

Start your itinerary with the "Getting to Know Torrevieja" section, which provides an overview of the town's history, culture, and geography. This foundation will help you grasp the context of the destinations you'll visit.

Discover Local Spots: The chapters "Authentic Local Experiences," "Culinary Delights," and "Cultural Hotspots" recommend locations to visit, eat, and explore that are popular among locals but are sometimes missed by tourists.

Outdoor Adventures: If you appreciate nature, see the "Outdoor Activities and Natural Wonders" chapter for suggestions on how to explore the area's natural splendor, such as hiking trails and isolated beaches.

Practical Tips: The "Practical Information" section includes important aspects including safety, transportation, and communication, guaranteeing a pleasant encounter.

Insider Insights: Don't miss the "Insider Tips" area, where we give vital information about the ideal times to visit, local customs, and sustainable travel practices.

This guide aims to help you make the most of your stay in Torrevieja. By immersing yourself in local culture and venturing off the beaten route, you'll obtain a better understanding of what makes this place unique.

What makes Torrevieja unique?

Torrevieja stands out for its diverse history, culture, and natural beauty. Here are some significant factors that contribute to its uniqueness:

The Salt Flats of Las Salinas: The town's history is inextricably linked to the salt industry, which stretches back centuries. The salt flats not only create a spectacular visual contrast with the blue waters, but they also play an important part in the local economy.

Today, they are a protected natural park that draws birdwatchers and nature lovers. You may explore the salt pans, watch the harvesting process, and learn about the role of salt production in Torrevieja's growth.

Diverse Cultural Influences: Torrevieja's cultural landscape is influenced by a variety of factors, including Spanish, Mediterranean, and international groups. The town's festivals, food, and traditions reflect its diverse population. From the bustling Semana Santa (Holy Week) celebrations to the lively summer fiestas, tourists may enjoy a variety of customs that highlight the town's history.

Natural Beauty: Beyond its beaches, Torrevieja is surrounded by spectacular scenery. The adjacent natural parks, such as Parque Natural de las Lagunas de La Mata y Torrevieja, provide hiking paths, birdwatching possibilities, and breathtaking views of the lagoons. These locations are home to a variety of species and are ideal for outdoor lovers wishing to experience the region's natural beauty.

Gastronomic Delights: Torrevieja's gastronomic scene reflects its coastal setting and agricultural riches. From fresh seafood to locally grown fruits and vegetables, the cuisine here is a celebration of flavor.

Traditional dishes from the town, including paella and tapas, can be found in local restaurants that are frequently hidden away from the main tourist routes. Discovering these hidden gastronomic jewels will give you an authentic experience of the region.

Torrevieja has a fantastic sense of community. The town is filled with friendly inhabitants who are proud of their past and eager to share it with guests. Engaging with inhabitants, attending local events, or simply conversing at a café can all provide insight into the town's personality and charm.

Sustainability Initiatives: As environmental awareness rises, Torrevieja is working to encourage sustainable tourism. Many local firms prioritize environmentally friendly practices, and efforts to safeguard natural resources are gaining popularity. By opting to use these sustainable solutions, you may enjoy your trip while also helping to preserve the area's unique ecology.

To summarize, Torrevieja is a place that provides much more than meets the eye. You'll discover the true soul of this coastal town by diving into its history, interacting with the locals, and uncovering its hidden beauties. This book is intended to be your entry point to a rewarding experience, enabling you to savor the rich tapestry of life in Torrevieja. Prepare to embark on a journey full of discovery, connection, and amazing memories.

CHAPTER 1: GETTING TO KNOW TORREVIEJA

1.1 A Brief History Of Torrevieja

Torrevieja has a fascinating history dating back to the early nineteenth century. Originally a small fishing community, it grew to prominence thanks to its salt business, which emerged as a critical economic force for the region.

The town's name, which translates as "Tower of the Sea," comes from a watchtower built in the 18th century to protect against pirate raids. This tower, known as the Torre del Moro, is a historic monument that still survives today, providing insight into the town's marine history.

Torrevieja's salt flats, known as Las Salinas, have long been its lifeline. They were first commercially exploited in the late 1800s, and by the mid-nineteenth century, salt manufacture had grown into a significant business. The growing salt trade drew residents and helped the town thrive. Torrevieja was officially formed as a town in 1830, and it immediately became a Mediterranean salt-producing center. This surge altered the local economy, as salt was a vital product both for preservation and trade.

Throughout the twentieth century, Torrevieja evolved. The introduction of the railway in the early 1900s improved transit and business, making the town more accessible. As tourism grew in the 1960s, Torrevieja's economy shifted from one based on industry to one centered on hospitality and leisure. This change was highlighted by the growth of hotels, restaurants, and recreational facilities to accommodate the growing number of visitors seeking sun, sea, and culture.

Torrevieja is now a popular tourist destination, noted for its beautiful beaches, bustling nightlife, and diverse culture. It has become a cultural melting pot, attracting both Spanish citizens and expatriates from other nations, particularly Northern Europe. This multicultural impact enhances the town's identity and adds to its vibrant atmosphere.

1.2 Geography and Climate.

Torrevieja is situated on the Costa Blanca, between the Mediterranean Sea and the national parks of La Mata and Torrevieja. This outstanding beachfront position provides stunning vistas and diverse natural settings. The town's landscape is defined by sandy beaches, rocky coves, and salt lakes, which provide a breathtaking backdrop for outdoor sports and exploration.

Torrevieja's climate is classed as Mediterranean, with hot, dry summers and warm, wet winters. Temperatures frequently exceed 30°C (86°F) throughout the summer months of June to September. The sun's warmth and moderate sea breezes provide a great atmosphere for sunbathing and water sports. Torrevieja is a sun-seekers paradise, with more than 300 days of sunshine annually.

Torrevieja's winter is quite moderate, with average temperatures ranging from 10 to 18°C (50 to 64°F). While there are periodic rain showers, the overall environment is mild, making it a desirable visit year-round. This favorable weather pattern allows visitors to enjoy outdoor activities year-round, such as hiking, cycling, and visiting the town's natural parks.

The town is also home to the famed salt lagoons, which are not only beautiful but also environmentally significant. The salt flats provide a unique habitat for a variety of bird species, including flamingos, making it a popular destination for birdwatchers. The magnificent landscapes that surround these lagoons offer several chances for photography and relaxation, allowing tourists to reconnect with nature.

1.3 Cultural Insight

Torrevieja's culture combines traditional Spanish roots with current influences, reflecting the town's rich history and diversified people.

Torrevieja's culture is noteworthy for its deep affinity to the water. Fishing has always been an important part of the local way of life, and the town's culinary traditions, festivals, and daily activities reflect this maritime influence.

The native cuisine is a lovely representation of Mediterranean culture, with fresh ingredients, robust flavors, and an emphasis on seafood. Traditional foods like paella, caldereta (fish stew), and tapas highlight the region's gastronomic heritage.

Visitors can eat these delicacies at local restaurants and tapas bars, which frequently have breathtaking views of the sea. The town's marketplaces, such as the Mercado de Abastos, are ideal for sampling fresh fruit, local cheeses, and cured meats, giving visitors a flavor of true Torrevieja.

Torrevieja is also noted for its vibrant festivals that honor the town's cultural past. One of the most important festivals is the Semana Santa (Holy Week), which features elaborate processions with religious floats and traditional music. The town's summer celebrations, such as the Fiestas de la Virgen del Carmen, honor the patron saint of fishermen with colorful parades, music, and fireworks. These events provide visitors with a one-of-a-kind opportunity to learn about and participate in local traditions.

Torrevieja's culture also has a strong emphasis on the arts. The town is home to several cultural organizations, including theaters, galleries, and museums that highlight the work of local artists and musicians. The Teatro Municipal de Torrevieja conducts a variety of performances, including plays and concerts, serving as a venue for artistic expression and cultural exchange.

Torrevieja's language and traditions reflect its mixed identity. With a large expatriate population, English, German, and other languages are widely spoken alongside Spanish. This linguistic diversity enhances the town's social scene and promotes inclusivity. Many local events and activities are geared towards international residents, creating a welcoming environment for guests from all walks of life.

Finally, Torrevieja embodies the spirit of the Mediterranean lifestyle, with a rich history, breathtaking environment, and thriving culture. Visitors may properly appreciate Torrevieja's uniqueness by learning about its history and participating with it today.

Torrevieja provides an authentic experience that will make a lasting impression, whether you're strolling through the lovely streets, sampling local cuisine, or taking part in colorful events. Prepare to be immersed in the warmth and charm of this coastal paradise as you discover everything it has to offer.

CHAPTER 2: ACCOMMODATION

When planning a trip to Torrevieja, it is critical to locate the correct accommodations to maximize your vacation experience. The town offers a broad choice of accommodation alternatives that accommodate to all budgets and preferences, from magnificent hotels to lovely guesthouses. In this chapter, we'll look at the best neighborhoods to stay in, recommend hotels and hostels, and highlight unique lodging options that offer an authentic local experience.

2.1 Top Neighborhoods to Stay:

1. La Mata

La Mata, located to the north of the town center, is known for its beautiful beach and laid-back vibe.

This neighborhood is great for those seeking peace and natural beauty. The lengthy stretch of sandy beach is flanked by palm trees and has a variety of attractions, including beach bars and restaurants. La Mata is also home to the La Mata Natural Park, where tourists may walk paths, see birds, and enjoy spectacular views of the lagoons.

2. **Torrevieja City Centre.**
Staying in Torrevieja's city center is an excellent choice for individuals who love to be close to the excitement. This dynamic district is packed with stores, cafes, and restaurants, making it simple to immerse oneself in local life. The Paseo Marítimo waterfront promenade has breathtaking views of the Mediterranean, making it ideal for strolls. Additionally, being centrally positioned allows you easy access to cultural sites, markets, and nightlife.

3. **Los Balcones.**
Los Balcones is a peaceful residential enclave located just inland from the ocean. This neighborhood is popular among families and long-term residents because of its tranquil atmosphere and close-knit community feel. There are several amenities available here, such as stores, parks, and restaurants. The proximity

to the town center and beaches makes it easy to explore while maintaining a more relaxing environment.
savouringiesta

4. **La Siesta**
La Siesta is another residential neighborhood recognized for its serene atmosphere and green spaces. It's a fantastic choice for guests who want to get away from the bigger tourist regions while being close to Torrevieja's center. This area has attractive villas and nearby parks, making it ideal for families and people wanting a more relaxed atmosphere.

5. **Los Locos Beach Area.**
Los Locos Beach is known for its bustling beach scene and energetic vibe. There are various bars, restaurants, and stores here, making it ideal for younger travelers or people who like to socialize. The beach is great for sunbathing, swimming, and water sports. Staying in this location puts you close to the action while yet providing easy access to more calm neighborhoods.

2.2 Recommended Hotels and Hostels

1. Hotel Playas de Torrevieja.

Hotel Playas de Torrevieja is a short walk from the beach and offers comfortable lodgings with beautiful sea views.

This family-friendly hotel has big rooms, a swimming pool, and an on-site restaurant that serves wonderful Mediterranean food. Its proximity to both the beach and the city center makes it a popular destination for tourists.

2. Hotel Torrejoven

Hotel Torrejoven, located near La Mata, is a wonderful alternative for those looking for a relaxing vacation. This beachfront hotel has modern amenities like an outdoor pool, fitness center, and restaurant.

Guests get immediate access to the beach and breathtaking views of the Mediterranean. The calm atmosphere is great for both families and couples.

3. **Hotel Laguna Spa & Golf**

For those wanting a touch of luxury, Hotel La Laguna Spa & Golf is an excellent choice. This hotel, located near the La Mata Natural Park, has a full-service spa, a golf course, and elegantly decorated rooms.

Guests can relax at the spa, dine at the hotel's restaurant, or explore the surrounding natural landscapes. It's quiet atmosphere makes it an ideal place for relaxation.

4. **Hostal La Playa.**

If you're traveling on a tight budget, Hostal La Playa provides economical yet excellent lodging in a prime location. This hostel, located just a few minutes walk from Los Locos Beach, offers clean accommodations and a welcoming atmosphere.

Guests can enjoy common areas, a bar, and easy access to nearby restaurants and stores. It's a wonderful alternative for backpackers and lone travelers wishing to meet new people.

5. **Hotel Marina Playa.**

Hotel Waterfront Playa, located near the waterfront, offers a pleasant setting while also providing modern conveniences. This hotel is ideal for individuals who want to stay close to the waterfront and enjoy water-based activities. With spacious accommodations and an outdoor pool, it's the ideal spot to unwind after a day of exploration. The on-site restaurant serves a range of local foods, enhancing the overall experience.

2.3 Unique Accommodations: Guesthouses and Rentals

1. **Casa de la Flores**

For a genuinely one-of-a-kind experience, consider staying at Casa de las Flores, a beautiful guesthouse in a quiet neighborhood.

This nicely designed property has wide rooms, a verdant garden, and a shared kitchen where visitors can prepare their meals. The kind hosts provide personalized service and insider information about area attractions, making it feel like a home away from home. It's a wonderful alternative for travelers seeking a personal and authentic experience.

2. **Villa Cielo.**
If you're traveling with a party or family, Villa Cielo is an excellent rental option that provides plenty of space and privacy. This beautiful house boasts a private pool, an outside terrace, and modern conveniences, all within a short drive of Torrevieja's beaches. The well-equipped kitchen makes meal preparation simple, and the wide living areas create a comfortable environment for relaxing. It's the ideal setting for making amazing memories with loved ones.

3. **Airbnb Options.**
Torrevieja offers a variety of Airbnb options to suit different preferences and budgets. Everyone may find something to suit them, from cozy studio flats near the beach to huge villas with sea views. Staying in an Airbnb helps travelers get a more intimate feel for local life, as the properties are often unique and beautiful. For an authentic

vacation, seek out ads that stress accessibility to local markets, parks, and cultural sites.

4. **Casa de La Sal**
Casa de la Sal, nestled on the salt flats, is another one-of-a-kind guesthouse choice. This eco-friendly lodging offers guests a sustainable experience while taking in the beauty of the surrounding natural environment.

The guesthouse has comfortable rooms, a community kitchen, and outdoor areas for relaxing. The hosts provide guided tours of the salt flats, explaining the history and significance of the environment. This stay blends comfort with a strong connection to the surrounding environment.

5. **Boutique hotels.**
Torrevieja is home to various boutique hotels that combine luxury and personalization. One such option is the Hotel La Fonda, which is recognized for its elegant decor and attentive service. Located near the town center, this boutique hotel offers convenient access to local

attractions while maintaining a cozy and intimate ambiance. Each room is distinctive in style and reflects Torrevieja's charm.

Conclusion

Torrevieja has a variety of hotel alternatives to suit any traveler's needs and interests. Whether you want to stay in a luxury hotel, a low-cost hostel, or a one-of-a-kind guesthouse, each option offers a unique experience.

You may make the most of your visit by choosing the proper neighborhood and type of accommodation. Prepare for an unforgettable vacation in this picturesque coastal town, where comfort meets authenticity and excitement awaits around every corner.

CHAPTER 3: AUTHENTIC LOCAL EXPERIENCES

Torrevieja is a town that combines vibrant culture and rich traditions, providing visitors with a variety of real local experiences. This chapter will take you on a journey through some of Torrevieja's most fascinating experiences.

From bustling markets full of fresh food to colorful community events that highlight heritage and the craftsmanship of local artists. Engage with the people, savor local flavors, and learn about the traditions that make this coastal town a hidden jewel in the Mediterranean.

3.1 Traditional Marketplaces and Food Halls

Torrevieja's traditional markets and food halls are excellent places to immerse yourself in local culture. These colorful establishments are more than simply grocery stores; they are active social hubs where folks come to shop, eat, and connect.

Market of Abastos

The Mercado de Abastos, or municipal market, is a must-see for any food enthusiast. This lively market in the town center sells a variety of fresh fruit, meats, seafood, and local delicacies. As you go through the stalls, you'll be met by the vivid colors of seasonal fruits and vegetables, the inviting perfume of cured meats, and the sight of freshly caught fish shimmering on ice.

Interact with friendly merchants, who are always willing to share their culinary expertise and offer the best local cuisine. You can pick up items to make a classic Spanish supper or buy some ready-to-eat tapas to dine on the beach.

The market also has modest bars and cafes where you can try genuine meals like jamón ibérico (Iberian ham) and queso manchego (Manchego cheese), served with a glass of local wine or beer.

Food halls and culinary experiences

In addition to the Mercado de Abastos, Torrevieja has several food halls that display the region's gastronomic offerings. Mercado del Mar, located near the waterfront, is a gourmet paradise that blends fresh seafood booths with restaurants serving delectable tapas and traditional cuisine. You can enjoy delicacies like fried calamari, grilled sardines, and paella cooked with locally sourced ingredients.

For a more immersive experience, consider taking a cooking class or taking a food tour around the neighborhood. Local chefs are ready to share their culinary secrets, allowing you to learn how to cook classic delicacies such as piste (a ratatouille-like dish) and tortilla española.

These activities not only teach you about Spanish cuisine but also let you connect with the locals, making your trip to Torrevieja even more unforgettable.

3.2 Community Festivals & Events.

Torrevieja is noted for its vibrant community spirit, which is brilliantly demonstrated by the numerous festivals and events hosted throughout the year. These festivals provide insight into the town's traditions and allow tourists to interact with the local culture.

Semana Santa (Holy Week).
Semana Santa, or Holy Week, is one of the most important festivals on the Torrevieja calendar. This religious ceremony takes place in the week preceding Easter and is distinguished by solemn processions that wind through the streets. Members of the local brotherhoods carry elaborate floats decked with detailed religious images, which are accompanied by melancholy music and the event's solemn mood.

Visitors can observe the community's deep commitment during these processions, which frequently feature dramatic reenactments and passionate expressions of faith. The town becomes a venue for these stunning events, offering opportunities for cultural absorption and reflection.

Feasts of the Virgin of Carmen
Another cultural highlight is the Fiestas de la Virgen del Carmen, which takes place in July to honor the patron saint of fishermen. This bustling celebration combines religious ceremonies and festive activities. The event begins with a colorful procession in which the statue of the Virgen del Carmen is paraded through the streets before being carried to the sea.

The celebrations continue with music, dancing, and delectable food, creating an electric atmosphere. Fireworks illuminate the night sky, and both locals and foreigners participate in the festivities, making it a joyful occasion full of camaraderie and cultural pride.

Torrevieja Carnival.
For anyone looking for a vivid and lively experience, the Torrevieja Carnival is a must-see. This funfair, held in February, is a colorful,

musical, and creative extravaganza. Participants dress in elaborate costumes and masks and parade around the streets in a stunning display of artistry. The event features competitions, live music, and dance performances, all culminating in a spectacular finale that embodies the spirit of joy and celebration.

The funfair is a fantastic opportunity to experience the local community's inventiveness and interact with other revelers. Visitors are welcome to participate in the celebrations, and many residents will welcome you with open arms, making it an excellent opportunity to engage with Torrevieja's culture.

3.3 Local Arts and Crafts

Torrevieja's local craftsmen and craftspeople help to define the town's cultural identity by creating one-of-a-kind products that represent the region's heritage. Exploring the work of these skilled individuals is a gratifying experience that teaches visitors about the community's workmanship and ingenuity.

Handicrafts and souvenirs.

There are several stores in the town center and along the beach promenades that sell locally manufactured handicrafts, jewelry, and souvenirs. These objects, ranging from handcrafted ceramics to superbly produced leather goods, provide a look into Torrevieja's artistic character. Many craftsmen are eager to discuss their stories and the skills that go into their works, giving visitors an understanding of the artistry involved.

Art Gallery and Studio

Torrevieja has various galleries that showcase the work of local artists. Galería de Arte Fina showcases a range of paintings, sculptures, and photographs inspired by the region's scenery and culture. Visiting these galleries allows you to participate in the local art scene, and you can often meet the artists and learn about their creative processes.

Workshops & Classes

To truly immerse oneself in local culture, try taking a workshop or class that focuses on traditional crafts. Many craftsmen provide hands-on experiences including pottery making, painting, and weaving. These workshops offer not only a one-of-a-kind souvenir but also the opportunity to learn a new skill while connecting with the community.

Conclusion

Torrevieja lives on real local experiences, such as crowded markets and vivid festivals, as well as the workmanship of its artists. Engaging with the community and immersing yourself in these cultural experiences will help you develop a better understanding of what makes this seaside town unique. Whether you're savoring the flavors of traditional meals, partaking in exciting events, or supporting local craftsmen, the experiences you have in Torrevieja will last long after you leave. Embrace the town's character and allow its rich culture to lead you as you discover everything Torrevieja has to offer.

CHAPTER 4: CULINARY DELIGHTS

Torrevieja is a gourmet wonderland, combining Mediterranean flavors with Spanish culinary traditions. With a diverse range of local specialties, busy marketplaces, and hidden gem eateries, the town provides a delightful gastronomic adventure for all visitors.

In this chapter, we'll look at must-try meals that capture the essence of the region, hidden gem restaurants where you can enjoy these flavors, and tapas bars that serve great snacks off the beaten route.

4.1 Must-Try Dishes: Where to Find Them

1. **Paella**.
No trip to Torrevieja is complete without indulging in paella, Spain's most popular meal. This rice-based dish is often prepared in a big,

shallow pan and can contain a range of foods such as fish, chicken, rabbit, or vegetables. Torrevieja's coastline location makes seafood paella a popular local dish, with fresh fish, prawns, and mussels.

Where To Find It:
Restaurante El Pescador: Located near the marina, this restaurant serves seafood paella created with fresh ingredients from the local market. Enjoy your meal while seeing the beautiful harbor.

Casa de la Paella: This restaurant is a local favorite, famed for its traditional cooking methods and large quantities. The paella here is a crowd favorite, and the boisterous environment makes for an unforgettable dining experience.

2. **Caldereta de Pesca**
Another popular dish to try is caldereta de Pescado, a tasty fish stew made with fresh fish, potatoes, and a variety of spices. This robust dish is frequently prepared with a tomato base and

seasoned with saffron, giving it a distinct flavor that recalls the region's seaside background.

Where To Find It:
La Taberna del Puerto: Located near the waterfront, this café has a cozy atmosphere and is known for providing excellent caldereta de Pescado. The dish is a menu mainstay that pairs well with a glass of local wine.

Restaurante Los Almendros: Known for its enormous quantities and genuine welcome, this restaurant serves caldereta de Pescado made from traditional recipes passed down through generations. The inviting atmosphere makes it an excellent choice for family dinners.

3. **Tortilla Española**
Tortilla española, or Spanish omelet, is a traditional dish consisting of eggs, potatoes, and onion. This simple yet excellent meal is a Spanish culinary staple that can be found in practically every tavern and restaurant in Torrevieja. The ideal tortilla is slightly thick and fluffy, with a golden exterior and soft, sensitive interior.

Where To Find It:
Cafetería Bar La Estrella is a popular spot for both locals and tourists, known for its delicious tortilla española. It can be served as a tapa or a main course, accompanied by a refreshing drink.
El Mesón de la Costa is a classic Spanish restaurant with a menu full of local specialties, including the delicious tortilla española. The cozy environment makes it ideal for a casual supper.

4. **Seafood tapas**
Tapas are an important element of Spanish culture, and in Torrevieja, seafood tapas reign supreme. From grilled octopus to fried calamari, these tiny dishes are ideal for sharing and offer a great opportunity to try a range of flavors.

Where To Find It:

Bar Restaurant La Tertulia: This vibrant bar is recognized for its broad tapas menu, which includes a variety of seafood dishes. The courteous staff is happy to recommend their favorites, assuring a memorable dining experience.

Restaurante El Rey de la Gambas: This restaurant specializes in prawn dishes and serves a variety of seafood tapas to highlight the freshness of the catch. The ambiance is lively, making it a popular destination for both locals and tourists.

4.2 Hidden Gem Restaurants

While Torrevieja has several well-known restaurants, some hidden treasures provide unique gastronomic experiences that are worth visiting. These lesser-known eateries are frequently situated away from the busier tourist areas, allowing you to enjoy real local flavors.

1. **Restaurante La Palmera**

Restaurant La Palmera, located somewhat inland from the beach, is a family-run restaurant renowned for its warm friendliness and homemade cuisine. The menu includes a variety of classic Spanish dishes, with an emphasis on local ingredients. Try their arroz a banda, a rice dish made with fish broth, or their luscious grilled meats. This restaurant's cozy atmosphere and good service make it a lovely find.

2. **Bodegón la Parra.**
Bodegón La Parra is a beautiful restaurant nestled away in a quiet neighborhood. This café specializes in local cuisine and delivers dishes crafted with fresh, seasonal ingredients. Don't miss the pimientos de padrón (fried green peppers) or pulpo a la gallega (Galician-style octopus). The laid-back environment and courteous staff make it ideal for a relaxing supper.

3. **Restaurant: La Casa de las Frituras**
Restaurante La Casa de las Frituras serves real fried fish. This tiny eatery serves freshly fried seafood with a choice of dipping sauces. The casual dining atmosphere allows you to enjoy your meal while socializing with the locals. Their fritura mixta (mixed fried fish) is a must-try, with a variety of seafood prepared to perfection.

4.3 Tapas Bars Off the Beaten Path.

If you want to eat tapas without crowds, there are various hidden tapas places in Torrevieja that offer a more personal setting. These businesses frequently provide distinctive food and a warm atmosphere.

1. **Bar El Pescaito.**
This small, inconspicuous tapas bar is recognized for its authentic atmosphere and ample serving sizes. El Pescaito specializes in seafood tapas, with grilled sardines and calamari being particularly popular. The relaxed atmosphere allows you to unwind and enjoy your meal, which is frequently accompanied by friendly conversation from the locals.

2. **Taberna La Oveja Negra**
Taberna La Oveja Negra, tucked away in a residential area, is a tiny tapas tavern with a cozy setting and an excellent range of local wines. The cuisine includes typical tapas like chorizo al vino (chorizo in wine) and gambas al ajillo (garlic prawns). The skilled staff is happy to suggest

wine pairings to complement your dining experience.

3. **Bar Los Cuatro Vientos.**

Bar Los Cuatro Vientos, located just off the major tourist trails, has a relaxed atmosphere as well as an extensive tapas menu. This pub, which specializes in homemade food, is a local favorite. Try their berenjenas con miel (fried aubergine with honey) for a deliciously sweet and savory combination. The courteous personnel and warm environment make it an ideal place to relax after a day of touring.

Conclusion

Torrevieja's gastronomic scene is a vibrant tapestry of flavors, customs, and experiences ready to be discovered. From must-try meals that highlight local seafood to hidden gem eateries that provide unique dining experiences, the town has something for everyone. Don't miss out on the thriving tapas scene, where you can sample a range of small plates featuring the best of Spanish cuisine.

You'll discover the genuine spirit of Torrevieja's culinary delights by exploring beyond the usual tourist hotspots and searching out local favorites. Embrace the flavors, engage with the people, and make great memories with the delectable cuisine that this coastal town has on offer.

CHAPTER 5: OUTDOOR ACTIVITIES AND NATURAL WONDERS

Torrevieja is not only a thriving coastal town, but also a gateway to breathtaking natural scenery and outdoor adventures. With a Mediterranean climate and different habitats, the area provides several chances for exploration and pleasure.

This chapter will take you through Torrevieja's stunning natural parks, less-traveled beaches, and scenic hiking and biking routes, making it a nature lover's and outdoor enthusiast's dream destination.

5.1 Exploring Natural Parks.

1. Natural Park of the Lagunas de La Mata and Torrevieja

The Parque Natural of Las Lagunas de La Mata y Torrevieja is regarded as one of the region's crown jewels. This natural park includes two big saltwater lagoons known for their ecological significance and magnificent beauty. The park is home to a diverse range of animals, particularly migratory birds such as flamingos, herons, and other duck species, making it an ideal destination for birdwatchers and nature photographers.

Visitors can explore the park via a network of well-maintained paths and observation sites that provide breathtaking views of the lagoons and surrounding terrain. The walking trails are appropriate for all ages and fitness levels, making it an ideal destination for families and casual walkers. As you go through the park, you'll learn about Torrevieja's unique salt production method, which has played an important role in the city's history.

In addition to birdwatching and photography, the park is a great place to picnic. Several designated locations offer tables and chairs for you to rest and enjoy the natural surroundings. The quiet environment and breathtaking surroundings make it a great spot to relax and reconnect with nature.

2. **Cabo Roig Natural Area.**
The Cabo Roig Natural location, located just south of Torrevieja, is another stunning natural location to visit. This coastal location is known for its craggy cliffs, beautiful bays, and crystal-clear waters. The impressive coastline offers plenty of options for exploration, whether you like to climb along the cliffs or rest on one of the quiet beaches.

The area also supports a varied range of aquatic life, making it a popular snorkeling and diving destination. Adventurers can hire equipment and explore the underwater realm, where colorful fish and interesting rock formations await. The views from the cliffs are breathtaking, especially at sunrise and sunset when the sky is painted in bright colors.

Cabo Roig is well noted for its walking routes that wind through the cliffs, offering beautiful views of the Mediterranean Sea. Keep an eye out for interesting rock formations and various vegetation while hiking. The peaceful surroundings make it an ideal respite from the hustle and bustle of town.

5.2 Beaches Less Traveled

While Torrevieja is known for its popular beaches, there are a few hidden gems that provide a more peaceful beach experience away from the masses. These lesser-known locations offer the ideal setting for leisure and exploration.

1. **Playa de la Mata.**
Playa de La Mata, located just north of the town center, is a gorgeous beach that is typically less busy than its rivals. The beach runs for more than two kilometers, leaving plenty of room for sunbathing, swimming, and beach games. The mild waves make it ideal for families with children, while the wide sandy shoreline allows for extended walks.

In addition to its natural beauty, Playa de La Mata has various beach bars and restaurants where you may enjoy refreshing cocktails and delectable seafood. The environment is relaxed, making it an ideal destination for people wishing to chill and soak up the sun.

2. **Cala Ferris**

Cala Ferris, located just south of Torrevieja, offers a more private beach experience. This little bay is flanked by rugged cliffs and thick flora, resulting in a stunning scene. The crystal-clear seas are ideal for swimming, snorkeling, or just resting on the beach.

Cala Ferris may require a short walk from the main road, but the tranquility and natural beauty make the effort worthwhile. Bring a picnic and spend a calm day by the sea, away from the congestion and bustle of the main beaches.

3. **Playa de Cura**

Although significantly more well-known, Playa del Cura maintains a more casual vibe than the area's busier beaches. The beach is furnished with sunbeds and umbrellas, making it a relaxing place to spend the day. The lovely seafront is lined with cafes and restaurants, ideal for a quick bite to eat or a refreshing drink.

What distinguishes Playa del Cura is its beautiful atmosphere and breathtaking views of the Mediterranean. Whether you're lazing in the sun or enjoying a leisurely stroll along the shore, this beach provides a pleasant respite.

5.3 Hiking and Bike Trails

Torrevieja is bordered by a variety of attractive hiking and biking paths suitable for outdoor lovers of all abilities. Whether you enjoy leisurely walks or strenuous excursions, there is something for everyone.

1. La Mata-Torrevieja Coastal Path

The La Mata-Torrevieja Coastal Path is a popular hiking and bike track with breathtaking views of the Mediterranean coastline. This trail is approximately 8 kilometers long and connects La

Mata Beach to Torrevieja's municipal center. The route is well-marked, with a combination of paved paths and natural trails, making it suitable for both walkers and bikers.

As you go down the path, you'll see lovely beaches, rocky outcrops, and stunning views. The calm sound of the waves and the fresh sea wind create a relaxing mood, making it an excellent choice for a leisurely outing. Along the walk, there are various benches and rest spaces where you may pause and enjoy the amazing views.

2. **Torrevieja Greenway.**
The Torrevieja Greenway is another great alternative for people wishing to get outside. This trail runs through the center of town and connects numerous parks and natural areas, making it ideal for walking, jogging, and riding. The well-kept path is bordered with trees and plants, offering a tranquil respite from the metropolitan environment.

This greenway is perfect for families and casual walkers since it provides convenient access to playgrounds, picnic spaces, and sports facilities. The route also includes informational signage about the local flora and fauna, which strengthens your connection to the environment.

3. Hiking through the Sierra de Escalona

For a more adventurous experience, visit the Sierra de Escalona, which is roughly 20 km inland from Torrevieja. This mountainous terrain has a variety of hiking trails suitable for all skill levels. The picturesque pathways wind across rocky environments, highlighting the region's varied flora and fauna.

Hiking in the Sierra de Escalona offers beautiful views of the surrounding valleys and mountains. The area is also abundant with wildlife, including several bird species, making it an ideal destination for birdwatchers. Pack a lunch and spend the day exploring this stunning natural location.

Conclusion

Torrevieja offers a plethora of outdoor activities and natural attractions, making it a great location for nature lovers and adventure seekers. From exploring magnificent natural parks and clean beaches to trekking scenic paths, there are numerous chances for exploration and recreation.

By immersing yourself in Torrevieja's natural splendor, you will obtain a better understanding of the region's distinct landscapes and ecosystems.

Whether you're taking a leisurely stroll along the coast, spending the day at a quiet beach, or going on a trekking excursion, Torrevieja's outdoor activities will leave you with lasting memories of this enchanting coastal town. Embrace the journey, connect with nature, and uncover the hidden secrets of Torrevieja's stunning landscapes.

CHAPTER 6: CULTURAL HOTSPOTS

Torrevieja is more than simply stunning beaches and scenic scenery; it is a thriving town full of cultural experiences that highlight its rich history, artistic expression, and dynamic community spirit.

In this chapter, we'll look at the local museums and galleries that recount Torrevieja's story, the theatrical acts and live music that bring the town to life, and the historical landmarks that offer a window into its history. Each of these cultural hotspots adds to the town's distinct personality and allows tourists to connect with its history.

6.1 Local Museums and Galleries.

1. **Museo del Mar y de la Sal (The Museum of Sea and Salt)**

The Museo del Mar y de la Sal is a must-see for anybody interested in Torrevieja's history and its relationship with the sea and salt business. The museum, housed in a lovely building that depicts traditional Mediterranean architecture, showcases a wonderful array of exhibits highlighting the town's marine legacy.

Visitors can look through displays of historical artifacts, photographs, and interactive exhibits that explain how important the salt trade was in the town's growth. The museum also highlights the significance of fishing and marine activities in the region, including traditional fishing methods and the numerous species caught in local seas.

One of the museum's main attractions is the exhibit dedicated to local aquatic life. Visitors can learn about the Mediterranean's unique ecosystems and the efforts to protect them.

The museum routinely holds temporary exhibitions, workshops, and educational programs, making it a dynamic location for both locals and visitors to learn about Torrevieja's cultural and environmental legacy.

2. **The Museum of Natural History**
The Museo de Historia Natural is a must-see for nature lovers. This small but interesting museum displays exhibits about the surrounding flora and animals, geological structures, and ecological systems. Taxidermy specimens, fossils, and interactive models help visitors learn about the area's natural past.

The museum's dedication to education is shown in its varied programs and guided tours, which are intended to engage both children and adults. By visiting the Museo de Historia Natural, you will obtain a better knowledge of Torrevieja's ecological value and the efforts being made to preserve its natural resources.

3. **Art galleries**
Torrevieja is home to various art galleries that highlight local talent and present a diverse range of artistic genres. Galería de Arte Torrevieja showcases shows from both new and recognized artists. The gallery presents regular exhibitions of paintings, sculptures, and photographs, giving

artists a platform to showcase their work to the public.

Furthermore, many of the local galleries take part in cultural events and art fairs, giving visitors a taste of the town's artistic life. Exploring the local art scene, whether you're an art lover or a casual observer, is a rewarding opportunity to engage with the community and admire the artistic expressions that capture the soul of Torrevieja.

6.2 Theatrical and Live Music

1. Municipal Theatre of Torrevieja

The Teatro Municipal de Torrevieja is the town's cultural hub, hosting a varied range of theatrical plays, concerts, and other live events. This magnificently restored theater, with its stunning architecture and small ambiance, makes an ideal venue for both local and traveling plays.

Visitors can enjoy a variety of performances, including classical plays, current dramas, and musicals. The theater also organizes dance performances, operas, and music concerts by both local and foreign performers. Torrevieja's dynamic programming reflects its artistic ethos, making it a must-see destination for culture fans.

The theater's calendar is full of activities all year, including special festivals and seasonal celebrations. Attending a play at the Teatro Municipal de Torrevieja is a great way to become involved in the local cultural scene and discover the community's skills.

2. **Live Music Venues.**
In addition to theater performances, Torrevieja has a thriving live music scene. Several restaurants and clubs around town hold frequent live music events including local bands, DJs, and solo performers. Torrevieja's music venues host a variety of genres, including flamenco, rock, jazz, and pop.

One famous venue is La Bodega de la Viña, a charming wine bar that frequently organizes live music nights. Enjoy a glass of local wine while listening to skilled musicians perform in a variety of genres. The intimate environment creates a comfortable ambiance, making it an ideal place to unwind after a day of exploring.

Another prominent venue is Café del Mar, which organizes regular live music concerts, especially during the summer months. This beachside pub has spectacular views of the Mediterranean and a lively environment, with acts ranging from acoustic to full bands. The mix of fantastic music, nice company, and stunning surroundings results in an amazing experience.

6.3 Historic Landmarks

1. Torre del Moro (Tower of Moor)

The Torre del Moro, often known as the Moor Tower, is one of Torrevieja's most distinctive monuments. This historic watchtower was constructed in the 18th century as an observation point to defend the coastline from pirate raids. The tower rises boldly on a rock overlooking the Mediterranean, offering panoramic views of the sea and its surroundings.

Visitors can stroll around the tower, which is encircled by beautifully designed grounds. The short walk up to the tower is worthwhile for the stunning views, especially after sunset. The Torre del Moro is not only a notable historical site but also a popular location for photography and picnics, making it an ideal destination for both families and couples.

2. **The Church of the Immaculate Conception**
Another famous sight is the Iglesia de la Inmaculada Concepción, a stunning church located in the town center. This church, erected in the nineteenth century, has spectacular neo-Gothic architecture and intricate stained glass windows. The inside is decorated with religious art and sculptures, resulting in a peaceful and quiet ambiance.

The church is an important part of the town, hosting numerous religious rituals and cultural activities throughout the year. Visitors are welcome to visit the church and its surroundings, and it frequently serves as the setting for local festivals and celebrations.

3. **Salt Flats in Torrevieja**
Torrevieja's Salt Flats are notable not just for their economic history, but also for their environmental relevance. These huge salt pans are a UNESCO World Heritage Site, famed for their gorgeous pink hues and diverse wildlife. Visitors can take guided excursions to learn about the area's centuries-old salt harvesting culture.

The salt flats are also home to a variety of bird species, particularly flamingos, making it a popular destination for birdwatching and photography. Torrevieja's salt flats are a must-see destination due to their natural beauty and historical significance.

Conclusion
Torrevieja's cultural hotspots provide several possibilities for visitors to connect with the town's rich history and artistic culture. Torrevieja is a cultural hotspot, with local

museums and galleries showcasing the region's history and inventiveness, as well as colorful theatrical performances and historical landmarks telling the tale of its past.

Exploring these cultural sites will help you better grasp the town's identity and the vibrant community that lives there. Torrevieja welcomes you to immerse yourself in its rich cultural tapestry, whether you're admiring art, witnessing a live performance, or visiting historical places. Embrace Torrevieja's cultural energy and let it inspire your own travels in this stunning coastal town.

CHAPTER 7: DAY TRIPS FROM TORREVIEJA

Torrevieja is not only a dynamic beach destination in and of itself, but it also provides a fantastic starting point for exploring the surrounding area. The area is rich in history, culture, and natural beauty, with numerous day trip possibilities for guests seeking to travel beyond the town's borders.

In this chapter, we'll look at adjacent towns worth visiting, beautiful drives and routes that highlight the Costa Blanca's stunning scenery, and nature retreats where you can immerse yourself in the region's ecological treasures.

7.1 Nearby Towns to Visit 1. Orihuela

Orihuela, located just a short drive from Torrevieja, is a medieval town with a rich cultural past and numerous architectural beauties. The majestic Catedral del Salvador, a beautiful Gothic-style cathedral built in the 13th century, can be seen in the town's center. Visitors can stroll down cobblestone streets surrounded by attractive plazas, cafes, and businesses that reflect the town's lively spirit.

Orihuela is particularly recognized for its stunning Baroque architecture, including the Palacio de Rubalcava and the Monasterio de Santo Domingo. In addition, the town has a significant literary past, as it was the birthplace of famed Spanish poet Miguel Hernández. Visit the Casa Museo Miguel Hernández to learn about the life and works of an important figure in Spanish literature.

A stroll around Orihuela's historic neighborhoods, notably the Barrio de Santo Domingo, is an excellent way to learn about the local culture. The town is easily accessible via automobile or public transit, making it an ideal day trip destination.

2. **Guadalest**
A day excursion to Guadalest, a lovely community high in the mountains about an

hour's drive from Torrevieja, offers a totally unique experience. This breathtaking area is known for its dramatic views, turquoise reservoir, and medieval castle. The community is surrounded by stunning mountain scenery, which makes for ideal photography and exploration opportunities.

The Castillo de Guadalest, an 11th-century fortification, is the town's main attraction. Hiking up to the castle provides panoramic views of the surrounding valleys and the breathtaking Embalse de Guadalest reservoir. The hamlet itself is beautiful, with tiny lanes filled with artisanal stores and cafes. Don't pass up the opportunity to sample local specialties and appreciate the slow-paced atmosphere.

3. **Altea**.
Altea, which is around 30 kilometers north of Torrevieja, is another wonderful town to explore. Altea, known for its breathtaking coastline views and classic whitewashed homes, is a popular destination for artists and creatives. Casco Antiguo, the town's ancient old area, with small

lanes lined with vivid bougainvillea, modest stores, and locally owned galleries.

Altea is home to the renowned Iglesia Nuestra Señora del Consuelo, with its blue and white dome. The views from the church's terrace are stunning, providing an ideal vantage point for admiring the shoreline. Spend the day exploring Altea's lovely streets, visiting art studios, and eating fresh seafood at a coastal restaurant.

7.2 Scenic Driveways and Routes

1. The Costa Blanca Coastal Road.

A picturesque drive along the Costa Blanca Coastal Road is one of the best ways to appreciate the area's natural splendor. This gorgeous route connects Torrevieja to the dynamic city of Alicante, with spectacular views of the Mediterranean Sea and mountainous coastline.

As you drive along the coast, you'll come across quaint seaside towns, secret coves, and breathtaking beaches. Stop in places like La Mata and Santa Pola to visit local markets, eat fresh seafood, or simply relax on the beach. The coastal route offers numerous opportunities for photography, particularly after sunset, when the sky is painted in bright colors.

Make sure to visit Cabo de la Huerta, a lovely coast with stunning views of the sea. The journey ends at Alicante, where you may see the famous Castillo de Santa Bárbara, which provides panoramic views of the city and coastline.

2. **Sierra de Espuña Natural Park.**
The Sierra de Espuña Natural Park is a must-see for mountain enthusiasts. This breathtaking natural location, about an hour's drive from Torrevieja, is ideal for outdoor enthusiasts. The park's meandering roads lead you through thick pine forests, steep mountains, and gorgeous valleys.

Along the route, you'll come across several views where you may pause and take in the stunning environment. The park also includes a number of hiking and biking trails, allowing you to immerse yourself in nature. Popular paths include Sendero de la Espuña, which provides breathtaking views of the surrounding surroundings.

The Sierra de Espuña offers a variety of outdoor activities, including hiking, biking, and picnicking.

7.3 Natural Escapes

1. The Salinas of Torrevieja

Don't miss out on visiting Las Salinas de Torrevieja, a one-of-a-kind natural environment noted for its vivid salt flats and rich species. The salt flats are a UNESCO Biosphere Reserve and provide critical habitat for migratory birds, particularly flamingos.

Visitors to the salt flats can join guided excursions to learn about the ancient salt harvesting method as well as the area's ecological value. The contrasting colors of the salt pans and glistening waters create a breathtaking visual spectacle. Birdwatchers will enjoy the opportunity to see a variety of species in their natural environment.

The area also has walking routes and observation points, making it simple to explore and appreciate the beauty of the salt flats. Visiting Las Salinas is an excellent way to reconnect with nature without traveling far from Torrevieja.

2. **Natural Park of La Mata Torrevieja**

The Natural Park of La Mata-Torrevieja is another great place for nature enthusiasts to escape. This large park is home to a variety of ecosystems, including salt marshes, lagoons, and sandy beaches. The park is home to a diverse range of bird species, making it a popular destination for birdwatching and photography.

Several pathways weave through the park, allowing visitors to explore the many landscapes and take tranquil walks in nature. The picturesque trails are ideal for hiking and biking, allowing you to enjoy the park's beauty at your own speed. Don't forget to bring your binoculars to see the local birds and admire the breathtaking views of the neighboring lagoons.

3. **Cabo Roig's Beach and Cliffs**
Consider visiting Cabo Roig if you want to relax on the beach while enjoying the scenery. This area has stunning beaches with smooth sand and clean waters, ideal for swimming and sunbathing. The nearby cliffs offer breathtaking views of the Mediterranean and are perfect for picturesque walks.

Cabo Roig is particularly recognized for its marine life, which makes it an ideal location for snorkeling and diving. There are various beach bars and restaurants where you may eat fresh seafood while admiring the breathtaking coastline views. Enjoy a relaxed day on the beach or explore the adjacent cliffs and hidden coves.

Conclusion
Torrevieja is a good starting point for discovering the region's diverse landscapes, beautiful villages, and natural treasures. With adjacent

towns like Orihuela, Guadalest, and Altea providing rich cultural experiences as well as breathtaking drives showing the beauty of the Costa Blanca, your day trip options are limitless.

Whether you're looking for historical discovery, breathtaking seaside vistas, or outdoor adventures, the Torrevieja region has something for everyone.

Embrace the spirit of adventure and allow the local towns, picturesque highways, and natural getaways to enhance your stay in this stunning region of Spain. Each day's trip promises new discoveries, cultural insights, and wonderful moments, making your trip to Torrevieja absolutely remarkable.

CHAPTER 8: NAVIGATING TORREVIEJA

Torrevieja's tiny size and diverse transport choices make it a pleasurable experience to navigate. Whether you prefer the ease of public transit, the freedom of biking, or simply exploring on foot, Torrevieja has many options for getting around and seeing the numerous attractions this coastal town has to offer.

In this chapter, we will look at the public transit choices available, highlight walking tours and bike rentals, and provide useful ideas for moving around Torrevieja efficiently.

8.1 Public Transport Options

1. Buses
Torrevieja has an effective bus network that connects it to neighboring cities and towns, making it convenient to explore the surrounding area. Grupo Subús operates a reliable, clean, and cost-effective local bus service.

The main bus terminal is in the town center and serves several destinations, including Alicante, Orihuela, San Pedro del Pinatar, and Murcia. Several local routes also run through Torrevieja, allowing residents and visitors to get between neighborhoods and famous destinations. Buses run frequently throughout the day; schedules are accessible at bus stations and online.

Tickets can be bought directly from the driver or from vending machines at the bus station. Check the bus schedules, especially on weekends and holidays, since frequencies may vary.

2. **Trains**.
Torrevieja does not have a train station, however adjacent Alicante and Orihuela do. The train infrastructure in this region is well-maintained and allows for convenient day visits to other cities. Alicante has easy access to a variety of coastal and inland sites, including Benidorm, Altea, and Murcia.

To get to the train terminals, use a local bus or taxi from Torrevieja. The rail services are frequently on time, and comfortable, and offer breathtaking views of the countryside and shoreline.

3. **Taxis and Ride Shares**

Taxis are widely available in Torrevieja and can be a convenient way to get around, especially if you are traveling with luggage or in a group. Taxi stands can be found around the town, particularly at the bus station, beaches, and shopping areas.

For a modern twist, rideshare apps such as Uber and Cabify are available in the region, offering a flexible and frequently less expensive alternative to regular taxis. These services let you order a ride using your smartphone, making them a convenient alternative for late-night trips or when you need to get to a certain place without bothering about public transportation timetables.

8.2 Walking Tours and Bike Rental

1. **Walking Tours.**
Walking is one of the greatest ways to explore Torrevieja. The town is tiny, with many of its attractions within walking distance of one another. Several local firms provide guided walking tours that highlight the area's history, culture, and natural beauty.

These excursions often include visits to significant locations such as the Torre del Moro, Iglesia de la Inmaculada Concepción, and Mercado de Abastos, as well as lessons on local traditions and customs.

Self-guided walking tours are also an excellent choice for individuals who like to explore at their own leisure. Several applications and other resources offer suggested routes and sites of interest, allowing you to design a custom itinerary. Don't miss out on the beautiful waterfront promenade, which runs along the shore and provides breathtaking views of the Mediterranean Sea.

2. **Bicycle Rentals**

Biking is an excellent way to see Torrevieja and its environs. The town boasts multiple bike rental shops that offer a wide range of bicycles, including city bikes, mountain bikes, and even electric bikes for those wishing for a more leisurely ride.

Biketribe is a popular rental store that offers low rates and well-maintained bikes. Renting a bike allows you to explore not just the town, but also the picturesque coastline pathways and neighboring natural parks. The La Mata-Torrevieja Natural Park is especially bike-friendly, with designated trails snaking through the stunning scenery and along the salt lagoons.

Cycling along the coast allows you to explore isolated beaches and hidden coves that are not easily accessible by car or public transit. Furthermore, it's a terrific way to be active while enjoying the fresh air and sunshine.

8.3 Tips for Moving Around

1. **Plan your routes.**

When traveling to Torrevieja, it is a good idea to plan your routes ahead of time. Learn about the area transit schedules, walking trails, and bicycle routes. Apps such as Google Maps can assist you in identifying the best directions and estimated trip times. Consider downloading a local transit app that gives you real-time updates on bus schedules and routes for increased convenience.

2. **Stay hydrated and protect yourself from the sun.**

Torrevieja has a Mediterranean climate, therefore summers can be hot and dry. When walking or riding, bring a water bottle to stay hydrated, especially during the warmer months. Wearing sunscreen, sunglasses, and a hat can also help protect you from the sun's rays while exploring.

3. **Be aware of peak tourist times.**

If you're traveling during peak tourist season (the summer months), be aware that popular sights, beaches, and transportation may be busier than normal. To avoid crowds, visit significant locations early in the morning or late in the day. This technique also allows you to have a more relaxing time while visiting the town.

4. **Take Advantage of Local Events.**
Torrevieja organizes a variety of local events and festivals throughout the year, providing a wonderful opportunity to immerse oneself in the culture and spirit of the community. When arranging your trip, check local calendars for events that may overlap with it. Participating in these activities can broaden your experience and provide a fresh perspective on the town's customs.

5. **Embrace Local Culture.**
When exploring Torrevieja, take the time to immerse yourself in the local culture. Engaging with the community will improve your experience, whether you're talking to shopkeepers, sampling local cuisine, or attending cultural events. Learning a few basic Spanish phrases can help you connect with others and respect their culture.

Conclusion

Navigating Torrevieja provides a multitude of options for guests to conveniently explore the town and its surroundings. Discovering this gorgeous coastal town is both convenient and fun, thanks to a dependable public transportation system, possibilities for walking tours and bike rentals, and helpful travel suggestions.

Torrevieja welcomes you to engage with its dynamic culture, gorgeous scenery, and kind people, whether you're taking a bus to visit neighboring sights, strolling along the promenade, or cycling through scenic routes. Enjoy the freedom of mobility and let Torrevieja's charm unfold as you explore this beautiful resort.

CHAPTER 9: PRACTICAL INFORMATION

Navigating a new destination entails not only seeing the sights but also knowing the practical aspects of travel. In Torrevieja, ensuring a safe and pleasurable stay begins with understanding important facts like safety tips, emergency contacts, money and payments, and language and communication. This chapter aims to provide you with the practical knowledge you need to make the most of your time in this thriving seaside community.

9.1 Safety Tips and Emergency Contacts

1. **General Safety Tips.**

While Torrevieja is generally a secure tourist location, it's important to stay cautious and take basic precautions to safeguard your safety.

Be Aware of Your Surroundings: As with any popular tourist location, be cautious of your surroundings, especially in crowded areas, markets, and public transit. Keep an eye on your stuff and avoid exhibiting anything important, such as expensive jewelry or electronics.

Avoid frauds: Be wary of frauds, especially ones that target visitors. Common scams include people soliciting donations, offering unwanted assistance, or selling products at exorbitant costs. If something feels strange, follow your instincts and walk away.

Stay Hydrated and Protect Yourself from the Sun: Torrevieja's Mediterranean environment may be hot, particularly in the summer. Drink plenty of water to stay hydrated, use sunscreen, and rest in shaded locations to avoid heat exhaustion or sunburn.

Know Your Limits: If you intend to participate in physical activities such as hiking or bicycling, be sure you understand your fitness level and the difficulty of the terrain. Always notify someone of your plans, especially if you're exploring less inhabited places.

2. **Emergency contacts**

Any traveler should familiarize themselves with emergency contact information. Torrevieja offers a variety of emergency services, and it is important to know who to contact in the event of an emergency.

Emergency Services: In an emergency, dial 112 for instant assistance from police, fire, or medical personnel. This is Spain's standard emergency hotline.

To report non-emergency problems, contact Policía Local de Torrevieja at 965 71 16 45. They can assist with minor events, theft complaints, and other safety concerns.

Medical Emergencies: If you require medical assistance, go to a nearby hospital or clinic. The Hospital Universitario de Torrevieja, located in town, can be accessed at 965 71 51 00. In addition, many pharmacies give basic medical aid and advice on mild conditions.

Fire Department: For fire-related situations, contact 080 or 965 71 40 64.

Ambulance Services: If you require an ambulance, phone 112 for immediate assistance.

3. **Travel insurance.**
While not an emergency contact per se, purchasing travel insurance is strongly advised when visiting Torrevieja or any other foreign destination.

Travel insurance can provide coverage for unexpected events such as medical emergencies, travel cancellations, and lost luggage. Be sure to carefully study the conditions of your policy and keep a copy of your insurance information with you while traveling.

9.2 Currency and Payment

1. **Currency used.**

The euro (€) is Spain's official currency. As of today, the currency rate may fluctuate, so check the current rate before traveling. Currency exchange services are readily available in banks, exchange offices, and airports.

2. **Exchanging Currency**

If you need to convert cash, try doing it at a local bank or authorized exchange office to avoid paying higher rates at tourist destinations. It is often recommended to convert money before coming or at trustworthy locations during your vacation.

3. **Credit/Debit Cards**

Credit and debit cards are generally accepted in Torrevieja, especially in hotels, restaurants, and stores. Visa and Mastercard are the most often accepted, however, American Express may not be accepted everywhere. When using a card, you may be asked for identification, so keep it available.

Contactless Payments: Many businesses in Torrevieja accept contactless payments, making transactions quick and easy. If you would rather not handle cash, be sure your card offers this capability.

ATM Access: ATMs are extensively available around Torrevieja, and you can withdraw cash in euros. When using an ATM, use caution; choose those that are well-lit and in high-traffic areas. Some ATMs may impose a fee for overseas withdrawals; thus, check with your bank before using an ATM.

4. **Cash payments.**
While many locations accept credit cards, it's still a good idea to have some cash on hand for smaller purchases, local markets, and institutions that don't accept cards. Typical prices for things such as coffee, tapas, and small souvenirs are frequently lower when purchased in cash.

9.3 Language & Communication

1. **Official language.**

The official language in Spain is Spanish (Español). The majority of Torrevieja residents speak Spanish fluently, and it is the primary language spoken on a daily basis. However, because of the town's reputation as a tourist destination, many inhabitants speak English, particularly in restaurants, hotels, and tourist attractions.

2. **Basic Spanish Phrases.**

Learning a few simple Spanish words can improve your travel experience and allow you to communicate with locals. Here are a few useful phrases.

- Hello: ¡Hola!
- Thank you: Gracias
- Please: Por favor
- Excuse me: Perdón / Disculpe
- Do you speak English?: ¿Habla inglés?
- Where is…? ¿Dónde está…?
- How much does this cost?: ¿Cuánto cuesta esto?

- I would like...: Me gustaría...
- Restroom: Baño

Locals appreciate the effort you make to communicate in their language, even if your pronunciation is not perfect.

3. Communication Options: Mobile Phones

If you intend to use your cell phone while in Torrevieja, check with your provider about international roaming charges before leaving. Many travelers opt to get a local SIM card upon arrival to get lower pricing on calls and data.

Local SIM Cards: You can get a prepaid SIM card from Movistar, Vodafone, or Orange from local stores or kiosks. This option gives you access to data and local calls without paying high international rates.

WiFi Access

Torrevieja provides numerous alternatives for Wi-Fi access:

Many cafes and eateries offer free Wi-Fi to consumers. Simply ask for the password when placing your order.

Public spaces: Some public spaces, such as parks or city squares, may offer free Wi-Fi, allowing you to connect while relaxing outside.

Accommodations: Most hotels and hostels include free Wi-Fi, making it simple to stay connected throughout your stay.

4. **Staying connected**
Consider downloading travel applications that provide real-time updates on local events, attractions, and transportation schedules. Apps like Google Maps, TripAdvisor, and local transport apps can be quite useful for navigating the area and learning what's nearby.

Conclusion
Having useful information at your fingertips will greatly improve your Torrevieja travel experience. Understanding safety precautions and emergency contact information, as well as how to manage currencies and payments and navigate language and communication barriers, will allow you to explore the town with confidence and enjoyment.

By being acquainted with these practical aspects of travel, you will be able to focus on making memorable experiences, connecting with the dynamic local culture, and discovering Torrevieja's own charm.

Whether you're lazing on the beach, eating wonderful tapas, or exploring the natural beauty of the surrounding area, being well-prepared will allow you to enjoy everything this lovely coastal town has to offer. Enjoy your adventure!

CHAPTER 10: INSIDER TIPS

Torrevieja may be a great experience, enhanced by its own culture, breathtaking surroundings, and friendly population. To make the most of your vacation, learn about the ideal times to visit, local customs and etiquette, and sustainable travel practices.

This chapter provides insider recommendations to improve your vacation experience and establish a meaningful connection with the community and environment.

10.1 Best Time to Visit

1. Spring (March-May)

Springtime is one of the greatest times to visit Torrevieja. With temperate temperatures ranging from 15°C to 25°C (59°F to 77°F), the weather is ideal for touring the town and participating in outdoor activities. During this time, the local flora blooms, bringing brilliant colors to the surroundings, particularly in the natural parks that surround the town.

Furthermore, spring is less congested than the peak summer months, making it easier to experience popular sights. Events like the Fiestas de San José in March and the Semana Santa (Holy Week) celebrations in April offer insight into local traditions and culture, making your trip even more unforgettable.

2. **Summer (June – August)**
Torrevieja's main tourist season is in the summer when travelers come to enjoy the sun, sea, and sand. Temperatures can get over 30°C (86°F), so remain hydrated and use sun protection precautions. The beaches are buzzing with activity, and several festivals and events take place, including the Fiesta de la Virgen del Carmen, which honors the patron saint of fishermen.

While summer provides a dynamic atmosphere, be prepared for greater visitors and increased lodging costs. If you like a more lively atmosphere and don't mind the heat, this season can be a great time to visit Torrevieja.

3. **Autumn (September–November)**
Autumn is another great time to visit Torrevieja, especially in September and October when the weather is still warm but more pleasant, with temperatures ranging from 20°C to 30°C (68°F to 86°F). The beaches are less crowded, and many people have returned to their daily routines following the summer rush, making for a more real experience.

The region's annual Cultural Festival in October features local music, dancing, and art, giving tourists a great opportunity to interact with the community. Autumn is an excellent time to walk in local natural parks because the temperatures are milder and the landscapes are still beautiful.

4. **Winter (December – February)**
Winter in Torrevieja is mild, with temperatures ranging from 8°C to 18°C (46°F to 64°F). Although this season may not be great for beachgoers, it is

wonderful for those who want to explore the town's culture and history away from the throng.

The festive mood is alive around Christmas and New Year's, with decorations, local markets, and seasonal festivities taking place all across town. Winter is an excellent season for a calm holiday, as many attractions stay open, allowing you to enjoy Torrevieja's attractiveness in a more relaxed setting.

10.2 Local Customs and Etiquette

Understanding local customs and etiquette can improve your stay in Torrevieja and encourage positive connections with the locals. Here are some crucial guidelines to remember:

1. **Hello**.
In Spain, greetings are warm and welcoming. A basic handshake is typical when meeting someone for the first time. Friends typically greet each other with a kiss on both cheeks. When greeting locals, use appropriate titles like

"Señor" or "Señora," followed by their surname (if known).

2. **Dining Etiquette.**
Dining is a fundamental part of Spanish society, and dinners frequently last several hours. Here are some dining traditions to bear in mind:

Lunch is normally served between 1:30 and 3:30 PM, while dinner is served later, between 8:30 and 11 PM. If you intend to dine at a restaurant, make reservations or expect a longer wait during peak hours.

Tipping is appreciated, but not required. In restaurants, it is typical to round up the bill or leave little change. If you receive excellent service, giving a 5-10% tip is a thoughtful gesture.

Sharing Food: Sharing meals is a frequent tradition in Spain, particularly when eating tapas. It is polite to wait for the host to serve food before digging in, and it is considerate to offer food to those at the table.

3. **Dress Code.**

While Torrevieja is largely casual, dressing adequately is recommended, especially when dining out or attending events. Locals dress carefully, and wearing beachwear outside of designated beach locations may be frowned upon. Smart casual clothes are generally welcomed in restaurants, particularly in the evenings.

4. **Public Behaviour.**

Spanish culture values courtesy and respect. Being respectful and utilizing "por favour" (please) and "gracias" (thank you) will help you build positive relationships. Avoid speaking loudly in public places, and follow local noise levels, particularly during nap hours in the afternoon.

10.3 Sustainable Travel Practices

As a Torrevieja guest, following sustainable travel behaviors benefits the environment while also improving your vacation experience. Here are some suggestions for traveling sustainably in the area:

1. **Use public transportation.**
Using public transportation, such as buses, trains, or rideshares, reduces your carbon footprint while touring the area. Public transport is generally more environmentally friendly than renting a car, and it allows you to get a better sense of the local culture.

2. **Support local businesses.**
When dining, shopping, or engaging in events, give priority to local businesses and markets. Supporting local artisans, restaurants, and stores guarantees that your contributions have a direct impact on the neighborhood. Seek out farm-to-table restaurants and local markets that highlight regional produce and products.

3. **Reducing Plastic Use**
Bring a reusable water bottle to help reduce plastic waste during your visit. Torrevieja has many public fountains where you can fill your

bottle with pure water. Avoid single-use plastics like bags and straws by bringing reusable alternatives.

4. Respect nature and wildlife.
When visiting natural parks and beaches, remember to "Leave No Trace." Stay on authorized trails, dispose of rubbish correctly, and do not disturb wildlife. If you enjoy hiking or bicycling, be careful of the environment and choose pathways with low ecological impact.

5. Participate in local conservation efforts.
Consider participating in local conservation programs or community events that promote environmental protection. Many organizations organize beach cleanups, tree-planting events, and educational programs. Participating in these activities allows you to give back to the community while meeting like-minded people.

6. Educate yourself and others.
Take the time to learn about the region's culture, history, and environmental issues. Understanding the context of your visit allows

you to interact more meaningfully with the community and share your experiences with others, increasing knowledge and appreciation for Torrevieja's unique environment.

Conclusion

As you plan your trip to Torrevieja, these insider recommendations will help you connect with the local culture, respect customs, and engage in sustainable activities. Understanding the optimum times to visit helps you to experience the town's attractions without the crowds, while familiarity with local customs ensures that your encounters with inhabitants are good and courteous.

Adopting sustainable travel habits helps to preserve Torrevieja's natural beauty and cultural legacy. Explore and connect with this gorgeous coastal town, generating lasting memories and enriching experiences along the way. Torrevieja welcomes you with open arms, and with this advice, you'll be well-prepared to immerse yourself in its colorful culture and stunning scenery. Enjoy your adventure!

CONCLUSION

As your voyage through Torrevieja comes to a close, it's vital to reflect on what makes this coastal town so unique. Torrevieja provides a one-of-a-kind experience that goes beyond the traditional tourist attractions, thanks to its breathtaking natural surroundings, rich cultural heritage, and friendly people. Embracing the local spirit and being connected with the community will not only make your visit more enjoyable but will also leave you with memorable memories that will linger long after you return home.

Embracing The Local Spirit
Torrevieja has a thriving community that takes great pleasure in its history, customs, and way of life. To completely embrace the local spirit, spend time interacting with residents, participating in local customs, and immersing oneself in the town's cultural offers.

Participating in community events and festivals allows you to experience the town's customs firsthand. Whether it's the colorful festivals of Semana Santa or the vibrant Fiestas de la Virgen del Carmen, participating in these events allows you to engage with people and learn about their traditions and beliefs. The upbeat atmosphere, complete with music and dance, allows you to rejoice with the locals and feel a sense of belonging.

Exploring the local food is another meaningful way to connect with the essence of Torrevieja. Indulge in traditional meals at family-owned eateries, and visit local markets for the freshest ingredients. Engaging with the people behind the food—chefs, sellers, and artisans—will help you appreciate the region's culinary heritage. Consider attending a cooking class to learn how to prepare traditional foods at home, allowing you to bring a taste of Torrevieja with you.

Furthermore, supporting local businesses and artists boosts the community's vitality. By shopping at local stores, dining at family-run restaurants, and participating in workshops led by local artisans, you not only enrich your own experience but also contribute to the preservation of Torrevieja's cultural fabric.

Staying In Touch with Torrevieja

Even when you leave Torrevieja, the connections you create there might last a long time. Consider methods to keep connected to the town and its culture after your trip ends.

To begin, stay in touch with the friends you met on your trip. Many locals want to share their culture and may be willing to stay in touch via social media or email. Sharing your experiences and memories can help to build long-term relationships and pave the way for future visits.

Engaging with Torrevieja online might also help you keep in touch. Follow local social media accounts, tourism boards, or community groups to be informed about local events, news, and activities. This connection can inspire future journeys, provide updates on festivals you might wish to attend, or provide information about the community's ongoing efforts.

Consider becoming an ambassador for Torrevieja by sharing your own experiences with friends, and family, and on social media. Promoting the town's beauty and charm helps to raise awareness and encourage people to visit this hidden gem. Sharing stories, images, and recommendations will not only help to preserve your memories but will also inspire others to appreciate Torrevieja's rich culture and natural beauty.

Finally, consider organizing a repeat trip. Torrevieja has a lot to offer, and each visit reveals new aspects of its beauty. Different seasons provide distinct experiences, ranging from beautiful spring blooms to sparkling holiday lights, guaranteeing that there is always something new to discover.

Final Thoughts
Torrevieja is a location that encourages discovery, connection, and appreciation. By embracing the local spirit and keeping connected to the community, you can create a more

meaningful travel experience that goes beyond sightseeing.

As you reminisce on your time in this charming coastal town, remember the friendly people, the flavors of traditional cuisine, and the breathtaking vistas that have captured your heart. Your trip to Torrevieja is more than simply a visit; it's an opportunity to immerse yourself in a unique culture and make lifelong connections.

Whether you're planning your next excursion or reflecting on your previous trips, remember that Torrevieja will always welcome you back with open arms, eager to offer its beauty and energy once more. Safe travels and great adventures as you continue to discover the world!

Printed in Great Britain
by Amazon